Amelia Earhart

by Barbara Spilman Lawson

Table of Contents

Introduction

In the early 1900s, airplanes were new. In 1903 the Wright brothers built a plane. The plane flew for the first time. Soon many people wanted to fly airplanes.

⌒ The Wright brothers built this plane. It flew 120 feet (36.6 m) into the air, but it flew for only 12 seconds.

In the past women were not allowed to vote. They went on marches like this one to try and win their right to vote.

In the past most pilots were men. Most women stayed at home. They did not work outside the home.

Amelia Earhart dreamed of being a pilot. She thought women could fly planes, too.

Chapter 1

The Early Years

Amelia Mary Earhart was born in Atchison, Kansas, on July 24, 1897.

When the United States was in World War I, Amelia wanted to help. She became a nurse.

↻ This is Amelia when she was seven years old.

Blanche Stuart Scott
First American Woman to Fly

In 1910 Blanche Stuart Scott became the first American woman to fly alone in a plane. But she flew for only a few years. She said, "There seems to be no place for the woman...flier."

Bessie Coleman

Bessie Coleman was an African American woman. She was not able to find anyone in the United States to teach her to fly. She got her pilot's **license** in France.

In 1920 Amelia and her family <u>moved</u> to California. There, they went to an air show. Amelia watched the planes in the sky. She wanted to ride in a plane, too.

Amelia worked hard to save money. She wanted to take flying lessons. Most flight schools did not teach women. But this did not stop Amelia.

Clue: The word <u>moved</u> has the inflectional ending -*ed*. It shows that the verb is in the past tense. Can you find more verbs with the inflectional ending -*ed* on this page?

In January 1921 Amelia met Neta Snook, a young woman pilot. Neta taught Amelia to fly a plane. Amelia learned quickly.

In December 1921 Amelia got her pilot's license. Amelia's mother and sister helped her buy her first plane.

Ⓤ Many people go to air shows. There, they can see tricks like this one.

Chapter 2

Amelia Flies

Amelia painted her new plane yellow. She called it the *Canary*.

Amelia set many flying records. On October 22, 1922, Amelia flew her plane 14,000 feet (4,267 m) into the sky. No woman had flown that high before.

↺ This is Amelia and her plane, the *Canary*.

Amelia wanted to fly across the Atlantic Ocean like Charles Lindbergh. A rich man named George Putnam helped Amelia. George Putnam loved flying and airplanes. In 1928 he paid for Amelia to fly across the Atlantic Ocean.

The Graf Zeppelin

In 1927 the *Graf Zeppelin* made its first flight in Europe. It was the largest airship ever built. It was 776 feet (263 m) long!

↻ This is what Amelia wore when she flew a plane.

The plane that Amelia went on was the *Friendship*. It left Canada on June 17, 1928. Amelia was with two other pilots. Amelia was very happy. But the two other pilots did not let her fly the plane. Amelia sat in the back of the plane for the whole trip.

The *Friendship* landed in Wales on July 18. Many people came to watch. They wanted to meet the first woman to fly across the Atlantic Ocean. But Amelia was not happy. She did not fly the plane herself.

Many people waited to see Amelia after she flew across the Atlantic Ocean in the *Friendship*.

Chapter 3

"I Want to Do It!"

Amelia set more flying records. During one flight, she flew 181 miles (291 km) an hour! Amelia flew faster than any woman pilot before her.

THE AUTOGIRO

On April 8, 1931, Amelia flew this aircraft at an **altitude** of 18,451 feet (5,624 meters). This aircraft is called an **autogiro**.

In 1932 Amelia married George Putnam. Amelia wanted to fly alone across the Atlantic Ocean.

Amelia left North America on May 20, 1932. Five hours later she flew into a storm. The plane began to fall. It almost crashed into the water!

Amelia landed in Ireland on May 21. She did fly across the Atlantic Ocean alone!

How long does it take to fly across the Atlantic Ocean?

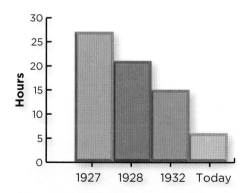

13

President Herbert ⮑
Hoover awarded the
National Geographic
Society gold medal
to Amelia after she
flew across the
Atlantic Ocean alone.

Amelia came home to the United States. People thought she was a hero.

In July 1932 Amelia set a flying record. She flew alone from California to New Jersey without stopping.

Canada

Pacific
Ocean

United States

Oakland,
California

Honolulu,
Hawaii

↺ Amelia flew alone
from Honolulu,
Hawaii to
Oakland, California.

Amelia decided to be the first person to fly alone <u>from</u> Hawaii to California. It was raining when Amelia left Hawaii. But that did not stop her. She flew from Hawaii to California in eighteen hours.

Clue: The word <u>from</u> is a preposition. A preposition comes before a noun or pronoun (*Hawaii*) and relates it to another word in the sentence (*fly*). Can you find other prepositions on this page?

↻ Amelia flew to Oakland, California alone.

Chapter 4

Amelia's Last Flight

In 1937 Amelia wanted to be the first person to fly around the world.

It would be a long, dangerous trip. Amelia chose Fred Noonan to be her **navigator**. He would help Amelia know where to go.

⋔ Amelia and her navigator Fred Noonan hold a map of the Pacific Ocean showing where they would fly.

Amelia and Fred left Florida on June 1, 1937. Twenty-one days later, they landed in New Guinea. Amelia was tired. But she did not want to stop.

Amelia and Fred left New Guinea on July 1. They were going to Howland Island. But they never got there. The United States Navy looked for the plane. But they didn't find the plane or the pilots.

↻ Amelia and Fred left New Guinea (1) to go to Howland Island (2). They may have crashed into the sea near Saipan (3).

 # Conclusion

Amelia Earhart's life was short. But she reached many of her dreams. Amelia showed that men and women can do many things if they try hard.

⌒ In 1963 the United States Postal Service made a stamp of Amelia Earhart.

Time Line of Amelia Earhart's Life

1897	◆	Amelia Earhart is born.
1920	◆	Amelia takes her first plane ride.
1921	◆	Amelia gets her pilot's license.
1922	◆	Amelia flies 14,000 feet high.
1932	◆	Amelia flies across the Atlantic Ocean alone.
1934	◆	Amelia flies from Hawaii to California alone.
1937	◆	Amelia leaves to fly around the world. No one saw her again.

Glossary

altitude   how high above the ground or sea level something is *(page 12)*

autogiro   a type of aircraft that looks like a helicopter. It goes into the air when wind spins the long, flat "wings" on top. *(page 12)*

license   a card or paper that gives a person legal permission to do or have something *(page 6)*

navigator   a person on a boat, ship, or aircraft who decides where to go *(page 16)*

Index

Comprehension Check

Summarize

Use an Author's Perspective Map to record clues about why the author wrote about Amelia Earhart. Then use the information in the map to summarize the book.

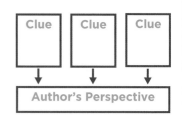

Think and Compare

1. Read page 15. Was Amelia brave? How do you know? *(Evaluate Author's Perspective)*

2. Would you want to become a pilot? Why or why not? *(Apply)*

3. Flying in a plane in the early 1920s was exciting. Do you think that flying today is also exciting? Explain. *(Evaluate)*